CYBER SECURITY

FOR BEGINNERS

How to Become a Cybersecurity Professional Without a Technical Background (2022 Guide for Newbies)

Shaun Kimmons

1

TABLE OF CONTENTS

INTRODUCTION 8

AUDIENCE TARGETED 10

WHAT'S INCLUDED IN THIS BOOK. 11

CHAPTER 1 13

SOFTWARE BUGS AND BUFFER OVERFLOW 13

.... 13

Error in calculation 13

Overflow of a buffer 14

The memory buffer's capacity 14

CHAPTER 2 18

WEAK PASSWORDS 18

.... 18

CHAPTER 3 21

HARDCODED PASSWORDS 21

.... 21

CHAPTER 4 23

NO ENCRYPTION 23

.... 23

CHAPTER 5 25

PATH TRAVERSAL 25

.... 25

CHAPTER 6 27

SQL INJECTION 27

.... 27

CHAPTER 7 29

CROSS SITE SCRIPTING 29

.... 29

CHAPTER 8 31

CROSS-SITE FORGERY REQUEST 31

.... 31

CHAPTER 9 33

VIRUSES & MALWARE 33

.... 33

CHAPTER 10 37

TROJAN & RANSOMWARE 37

.... 37

CHAPTER 11 39

ROOTKITS & WORMS 39

.... 39

Rootkits are another type of malware. 39

Worms. 40

....40

Adware. 41

....41

CHAPTER 12 42

DOS ATTACKS 42

.... 42

Denial of Service (DoS) attack. 42

CHAPTER 13 44

MAN-IN-THE-MIDDLE ATTACKS 44

.... 44

CHAPTER 14 46

SOCIAL ENGINEERING AND PHISHING ATTACKS 46

.... 46

Website forgery..49

CHAPTER 15 50

MITIGATE PHISHING ATTACKS 50

.... 50

CHAPTER 16 53

CLOUD SERVICES ATTACKS 53

.... 53

CHAPTER 17 56

SECURITY INTELLIGENCE BASICS 56

.... 56

CHAPTER 18 59

AUTHORING THE INTELLIGENCE................................... 59

.... 59

CHAPTER 19 63

ARP POISONING 63

.... 63

CHAPTER 20 66

ROGUE ACCESS POINTS 66

.... 66

CHAPTER 21 69

MAN IN THE MIDDLE ON WIRELESS NETWORKS 69

.... 69

Attacks Based on Misconceptions 70

CHAPTER 22 72

DE-AUTHENTICATION ATTACK 72

.... 72

CHAPTER 23 74

WIRELESS COLLISION ATTACK 74

.... 74

CHAPTER 24 76

WIRELESS REPLAY ATTACKS 76

.... 76

CHAPTER 25 78

PROTECTING WIRELESS NETWORKS 78

.... 78

BONUS CHAPTER VPN CONCEPTS.................................... 81

INTRODUCTION

The tools I'll describe in this book can be used for both white hat and black hat hacking.

When applied, the result will be the same in both cases.

Nonetheless, it can result in a disastrous situation for the person who uses such hacking tools in an unauthorized manner, which may cause system damage or a system outage.

Anything that is legally permitted to assist people or businesses in identifying vulnerabilities and potential risks is acceptable.

All of the tools I'll describe should only be used to improve your security posture.

I feel compelled to issue a warning here.

If you want to learn about hacking and penetration testing, it's best to set up a home lab and practice using these tools in an isolated network that you have complete control over and that isn't connected to any production environment or the internet.

If you use these tools for black hat purposes and get caught, it will be entirely your fault, and no one will hold you accountable.

So, once again, I strongly advise you to stay within the lines, and anything you do should be completely legal and authorized.

If you attempt to use any of these tools on a network without authorization and disrupt or damage any systems, you are engaging in illegal black hat hacking.

As a result, I would like to encourage all readers to only use the tools described in this book for white hat purposes.

Finally, if you are unsure about anything you are doing and have no idea what the outcome will be, consult your manager or do not do it.

This book is intended for educational purposes.

It is intended for those who want to become IT professionals or white hat hackers and are interested in learning and understanding what is going on behind the scenes.

In addition to legal concerns, it is recommended that you have a basic understanding of networking concepts before using any of the tools.

AUDIENCE TARGETED

This book is intended for anyone who wants to work as an IT Professional, specifically in the field of information security. The book is written in simple English with no technical background necessary even If you're new to information technology .The contents of this book will provide a high level of information security.An overview of network and wireless security on a high level. If you're getting ready,to work as an IT Professional, such as an Ethical Hacker or an IT Security AnalystAnalyst, Information Technology Security Engineer, Network Analyst, Network Engineer, ora Cybersecurity Specialist, but are still unsure and want to learn more about.You will find this book extremely useful if you are interested in network security. You are going to learn important network concepts and methodologiesYou should be concerned about security as well as key technologies. If you are serious about becoming a Cybersecurity Specialist, this is the place to be.This book is for you.

Assuming you are studying to become a teacher,This book will undoubtedly benefit information security professionals.Great information that will help you as you enter this industry .This book's contents revolve around a variety of topics, includingThe security mindset, as well as daily security tasks and activities, are important, but the main The purpose of this book is to assist you in understanding the most common System intrusions, as well as network security

WHAT'S INCLUDED IN THIS BOOK.

There are a variety of threats out there that you should be aware of, as well as how to mitigate them.

This can be done manually or automatically using security appliances or APIs.

This book will teach you about these threats and how to mitigate them, whether through security intelligence or automation.

Some of the major topics we will cover include the types of threats that can affect organizations regardless of whether the devices are on-premises or in the cloud, what security intelligence is and what solutions we have for it, and how to use APIs to interact with certain security appliances.

By the end of book 1, you'll understand how to identify threats to your network and mitigate them with some of the industry's best security tools.

This book will cover a variety of security threats that commonly target organizations' IT infrastructures.

If you're reading this, I'd like to welcome you to your journey of learning about these threats and the solutions we can offer.

This book is for you if you want to work as a network or security administrator.

If you work in IT or want to change careers in IT, this book will teach you about the security threats that you should be aware of.

While you do not need to be a computer programmer by trade, basic networking knowledge is highly recommended.

Assume you are a network engineer, and the CIO (Chief Information Officer) has assigned you the task of learning about the various threats that may affect your company's network.

Regardless of whether the devices are on-premises or in the cloud.

Because your company is thinking about using a security intelligence solution to help protect against these threats, you've been tasked with learning how it works.

The chapters that follow will introduce you to the various threats that may affect your company's IT networks.

First, I'll expand on that knowledge by discussing the various threats that affect on-premises environments, as well as threats that affect cloud environments.

In addition, I will discuss how social engineering and phishing can have a significant impact on both the company and individual people.

CHAPTER 1

SOFTWARE BUGS AND BUFFER OVERFLOW

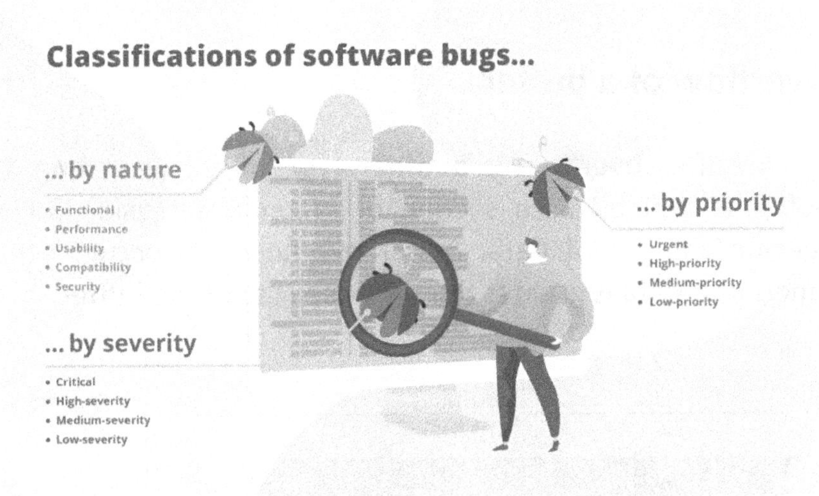

The first vulnerability I'd like to discuss with you is software bugs. A software bug is simply a flaw in a computer program.This causes a program to behave unexpectedly. ThisIt could be as simple as a flaw in the software's logic.

Error in calculation

For instance, suppose an excel spreadsheet is supposed to take the contents of two cells, add them together and store the result in a third cell, but instead adds the values together rather than multiplying them.When you combine them, you will get unexpected results. This is known as a calculation error.

The third cell should contain the results that you expect.The product of the previous two cells Because the application did not do what it was supposed to do.That is an example of a bug, as the person who wrote it intended.

Overflow of a buffer

A buffer overflow is another type of software bug. A buffer is defined as a section of memory set aside for a specific amount of data. Buffer overflow can occur if the amount of data is greater than the capacity of the buffer.

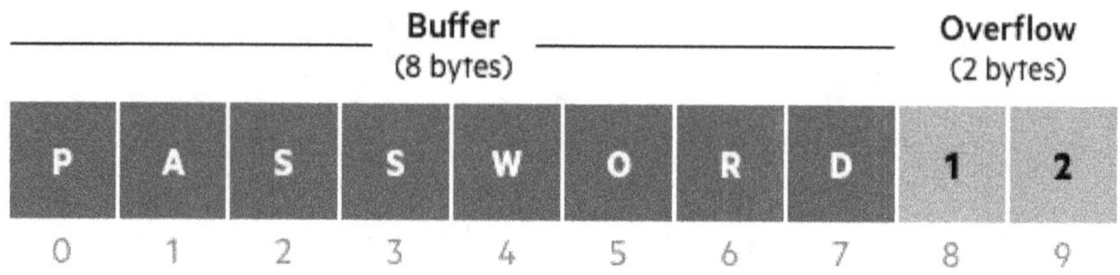

The memory buffer's capacity

A form is an example of this occurring outside of computers that you may have provided information on a form, such as your name and address, and there are a few rows of boxes on the form.When filling out these forms, you are only supposed to fill in the blanks.Each box should contain one letter or one number. If you happen to own a longer last name than the form's designer made room for.

for example, you would go over the amount of space when filling out the form reserved for the use of your surname.This creates ambiguity. What is the proper place to put your first name? Do you think so?

Just leave a space and continue? What if that takes too long?trespass on the space of the next box? Will the person who reads the form.I believe you meant to write over the box in the other section.

Similarly, when a computer's software writes to memory.In addition to the stack, the software makes use of buffers to store various data.inside one's memory, These buffers are positioned next to one another.As a result, if each buffer contains multiple different values, andEach buffer has a set number of bits that will be used to hold the data, similar to a form that contains a specific number of boxes for the last name, address, and so on, similar to the form, if there was one.The more data that is placed inside the buffer than there is space for, the Data in the following buffer may be overwritten.You may be wondering, "Why is this important for me to know?"about trivial matters such as spreadsheets that aren't working properly or data that is larger than the buffer set aside for it?True, in most cases, the worst that can happen withThe purpose of software bugs is to cause frustration, and more often than not,The bug is completely unnoticed.

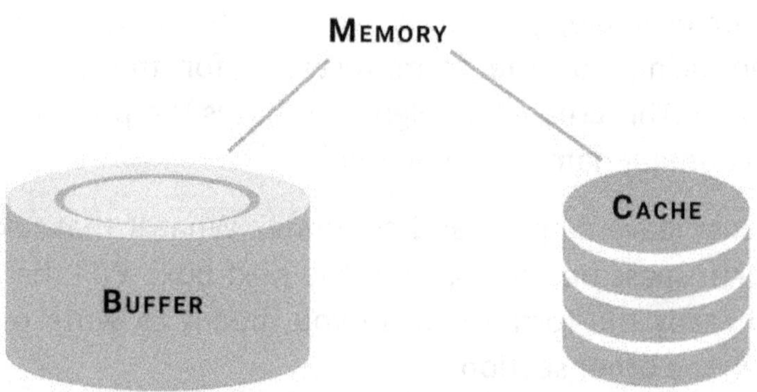

However, you should be aware that malicious attackers can exploit.These bugs are used to manipulate programs so that they do what they want.Rather than a minor annoyance caused by the program not working properly,that it was designed to do, a skilled attacker could exploit their knowledgeof the bug and exploit it in a way that will benefit them.A skilled attacker, for example, could exploit a buffer overflow and obtain information that they would not have been able to obtain otherwise They are even capable of write over their original data so that it no longer contains the same informationor they could take advantage of the buffer overflow tocause a host on which the software was running to crash, resulting in a Denial of Service (DoS) attack.

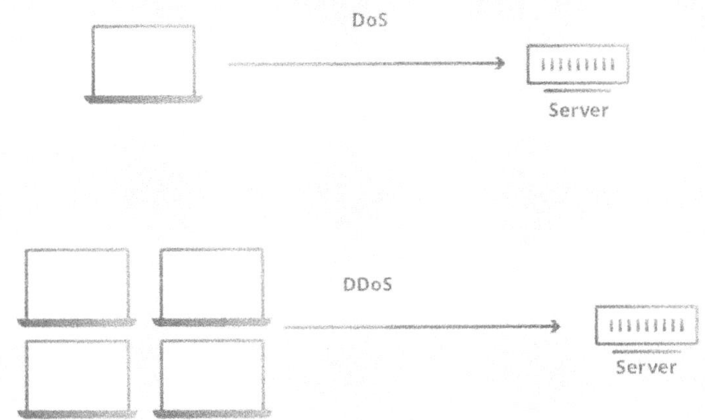
DoS
Server
DDoS
Server

CHAPTER 2

WEAK PASSWORDS

Passwords are used to restrict access to sensitive data that only certain people or programs should have access to. Certain criteria must be met for the passwords to be effective. One of the requirements is that the password is strong. A password must be both complex and long to be considered strong. The longer the password, the more difficult it is for brute force attacks to crack it.

Passwords used to only need to be eight characters long to be considered secure. According to research, a minimum of 12 or 16 characters is required. Password complexity is also important. Just as each additional character makes a password more secure, increasing the type of character that can be used makes it more difficult for a password cracker program to obtain the final password. For example, if you create a password that is eight characters long and only contains upper and lowercase letters, there are over 53 trillion possible password combinations. When numeric characters such as 0 through 9 are added, there are now 62 options for each character, bringing the total number of possible combinations to more than 218 trillion. Finally, allowing special characters increases the number of options for each character to 74, bringing your 8-character password to nearly 900 trillion options. While all of these numbers appear to be so large that it would take a millennium to crack, the truth is that even with nearly 900 trillion combinations, it would only take today's computers 2 and a half hours to crack.

The 8-character password made up of only upper and lowercase letters would take only 9 minutes to crack. If we increase the number of characters in the password from 8 to 12, the total number of passwords using only upper and lowercase letters increases from 53 trillion to over 390 quintillions. A quintillion is a billion times a billion. The time it would take to crack a password consisting only of upper and lowercase letters is more impressive than the size of that number. It would take today's computers 123 years to crack that password. Including numbers and special characters increases the number of possible combinations to 26 sextillion, which is a quintillion time 1,000. And that password goes from taking 123 years to over 8500 years to crack. The length and complexity of the password aren't the only factors that contribute to its strength. Passwords should not contain any dictionary words, names, or important dates. Because password crackers are preloaded with dictionary words to try first, using a dictionary word can transform your 12-digit password from taking 8500 years to being cracked instantly.

Names and important dates also make it easier to guess passwords because they are easier to figure out. After all, they are important to you. Furthermore, add a special character at the end of your password by using the $ sign instead of an S, a 3 instead of an E, a @ instead of an A, and a 0 instead of an O or an exclamation mark do not provide additional security. While this may have worked in the past, password crackers now include libraries that include these letter replacements. To protect against weak passwords, include requirements that passwords expire after a certain period and that any previously used passwords be excluded.

CHAPTER 3

HARDCODED PASSWORDS

Hardcoded passwords are another security risk associated with passwords. Passwords that are hardcoded are passwords that are embedded in various applications.

The password could be either an inbound or outbound variant. In the inbound variant, to gain administrative access to the program, the credentials that were provided are checked against a set of hardcoded credentials. When the application needs to connect to another device or service, the outbound variant is used. In the original application, the password for connecting to that device or service is hardcoded. The problem with either of these variants is that an attacker can easily obtain the password by examining the source code or binary export of the code. Once the attacker has obtained the password, they can access all programs that use the same password. If the software is installed on multiple devices, the attacker can compromise all of them with a single password. There are a few options for protecting against hardcoded passwords. One option is to keep passwords separate from the code in a configuration file that is strongly encrypted and protected. Rather than having a hardcoded default username and password, the program could simply prompt the user to create a password upon first login. If the software must contain hardcoded credentials, another mitigation is to use strong one-way hashes and store those hashes in the configuration file. The hash of the entered password would then be compared to the configured password by the program. This is advantageous because even if the attacker gains access to the configuration file, they will still have to try to crack the passwords, and if the passwords are strong, as discussed previously, it will take the attacker thousands of years to crack the password.

CHAPTER 4

NO ENCRYPTION

Encryption is essential in today's world for sensitive data. Encrypting the data ensures its confidentiality and integrity.

Encryption can be used for both data in transit and data at rest. When connecting to websites, for example, it is common to practice using HTTPS, which creates a tunnel using TLS. Because the communication is encrypted, anyone who can see the communication between the client and the server is unable to see the actual payload of the data. It is equally important to encrypt data at rest. Encrypting files and other sensitive data makes it much more difficult for an attacker to gain unauthorized access to information. Furthermore, it makes it much more difficult for an attacker to manipulate data. If the encryption is missing from the data, the data is exposed. For example, if a program saves a user's credentials to a cookie for faster login to a website, but that cookie does not encrypt the password, the credentials would be very easy to figure out if the system was ever compromised. As you can see, these are just a few examples of how not using encryption poses a serious security risk.

CHAPTER 5

PATH TRAVERSAL

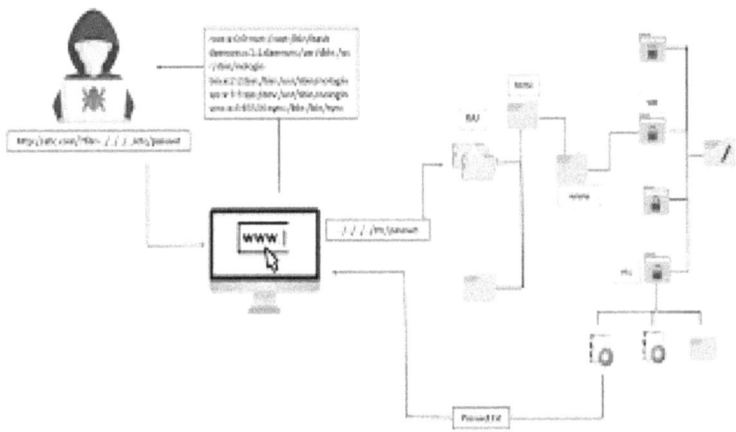

Path traversal is another type of security flaw. This vulnerability occurs when an application allows a malicious actor to navigate outside of the directory that the user is presented with.

For example, if the attacker was on a web page and wanted to try to browse around to find different files, they could use a path traversal attack to do so. When the attacker is on a legitimate web page, they can try to navigate to different files by typing "../" to navigate up a directory or an encoding that represents the by typing ".. / %2e %2e %2f". If the website is vulnerable to attack, the attacker could quickly figure out the directory structure with a few guesses, as well as by using the webserver returning errors about the file structure. Once the directory structure has been compromised, the attacker can browse various files such as the password file, system files, and other unauthorized data. To protect against path traversal attacks, websites should try to work without user input when using file system calls. Another prevention mechanism is to ensure that the user's input is validated by blacklisting all entries, except known good ones, such as special characters. Another good mitigation technique is for the administrator to use indexes rather than the actual names of the file locations. So, rather than having the user type in Alaska to navigate to the Alaska directory, have them use an id such as 20.

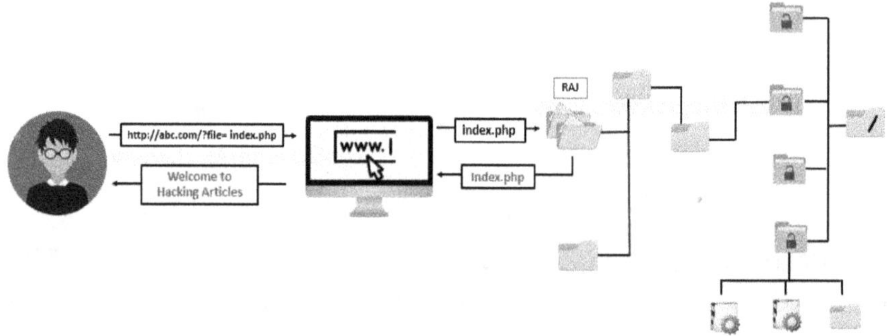

CHAPTER 6

SQL INJECTION

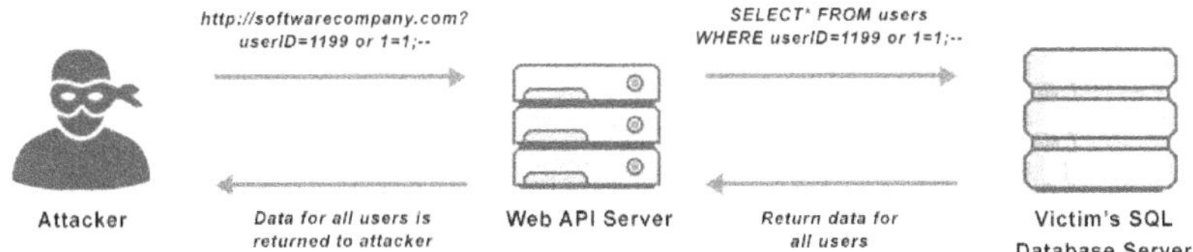

An SQL injection attack is another security flaw that can affect web applications. A SQL injection attack is one in which additional code is injected into the original SQL code.

Essentially, it allows the attacker to add additional code to achieve their goals. SQL injections are important to understand for a variety of reasons. First and foremost, they are easily discovered. A quick web search will reveal several vulnerable sites. Furthermore, SQL injections are common and easy to export, although the impact of SQL injections can be severe. In terms of impact, consider what can happen if a SQL injection is successful. The SQL injection attack, for example, has the potential to gain access to confidential data. Data such as usernames and passwords, personally identifiable information, social security numbers, home addresses, or sensitive corporate records such as bank accounts, profit and loss statements, or even intellectual property can be accessed with a successful SQL injection attack. Once the SQL injection has access to the data, it can modify it. This has an impact on data integrity because it is impossible to know whether or not the data is accurate once the attack has occurred. Some attacks may even initiate the creation of additional accounts for the attacker to use to gain even more access or the creation of fake information that could be harmful to the organization. Another effect is the original system's availability. If the attacker can manipulate the data using SQL injection, they may be able to delete critical data, rendering the system inoperable. They could, for example, delete all of the records stored in the database, rendering the database useless. The attacker could even go a step further and delete critical files required for the database or the operating system that the database runs on to function properly. In any case, the database isn't working the way it was intended to.

CHAPTER 7

CROSS SITE SCRIPTING

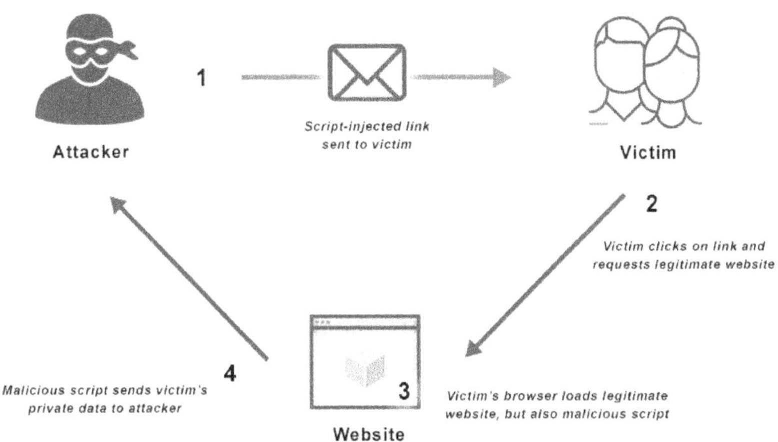

Cross-site scripting, abbreviated as XSS. When a malicious user injects malicious code or scripts into a legitimate website, this is referred to as XSS. For the website to behave as the attacker desires, the attacker uses untrusted data, which is user input that websites use as a search function. A malicious attacker, for example, could write code, such as JavaScript, that would run in the search function. The attacker inserts malicious code into a link to a legitimate website. If the attacker then convinces a user to click on that link, the code will be executed on that user's machine. JavaScript code can easily send the attacker the user's cookie data, which may contain usernames and passwords for various sites. The attacker can use various tools, such as a URL shortener, to make a link display only the legitimate website while concealing the malicious code behind it. A persistent XSS can also be used by the attacker to change the code on the server-side. Once the code is saved on the server, it's easy to imagine the various types of security flaws that the attacker could exploit on unsuspecting website visitors. They can have their code permanently saved to a benign website, so that when legitimate user traffic navigates to the site, the attacker's code runs, even if the user did not click on the attacker's malicious link. Using the security encoding library is one of the best ways to protect against cross-site scripting. This prevents attackers from using various escaping shortcuts to run their code. Another preventative measure is to properly design the web page by not allowing untrusted data within specific areas of HTML, JavaScript, CSS, or other coding languages.

CHAPTER 8

CROSS-SITE FORGERY REQUEST

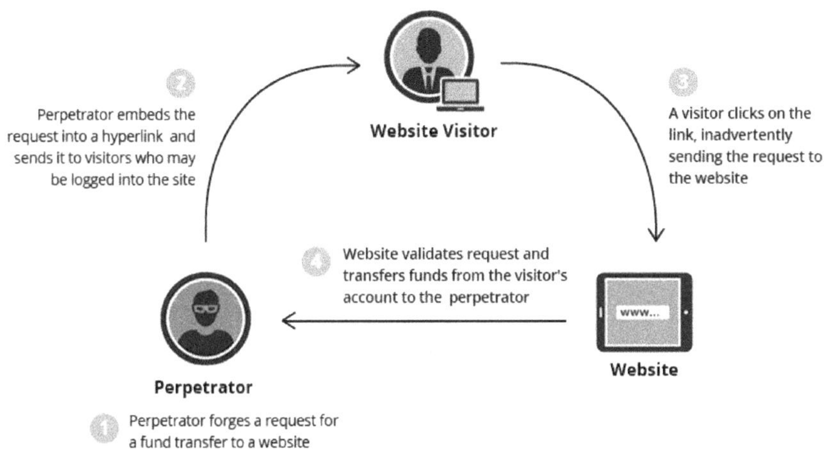

By forging a cross-site request, an attacker can take advantage of legitimate cross-site requests and force the victim's computer to perform unwanted actions on websites to which they have already authenticated. For example, if an attacker successfully social engineers a user into clicking on a link, or replants the link in an otherwise legitimate site, the script will run and force the user to perform an unwanted action. If a banking website uses a get request to transfer money from one member to another, an attacker can change the URL to transfer money to themselves. This URL is easily concealed by using a URL shortener or embedding the link within a different name. Cross-site scripting mitigations are recommended to protect against cross-site forgery. While XSS is not required for a successful cross-site forgery attack, cross-site forgery mitigations can be circumvented with a successful cross-site scripting attack. Once cross-site scripting has been addressed, cross-site forgery requests can be addressed by employing secure random tokens. Users can also help to protect themselves by using a browser that supports SameSite cookie attributes. Even if the link is legitimate, this will prevent the browser from sending the cookie.

CHAPTER 9

VIRUSES & MALWARE

We've already discussed the various types of security flaws that can affect today's networks. Now it's time to move on, expand on that knowledge, and discuss different threats that can affect both on-premises networks and cloud-based network environments. In particular, we'll go over some additional threats that you should be aware of to protect your company's on-premises IT equipment. The course will then go over Denial of Service and man-in-the-middle attacks.

Following that, you will learn about social engineering and how phishing is a common social engineer attack. After you've learned about phishing, you'll understand how the endpoint can help the user and prevent a successful phishing attack. Following that, we will go over specific threats that can affect your company's cloud-based IT infrastructure. As a security engineer, you must be aware of the various digital threats that attackers can use to disrupt legitimate business activity. Enterprise IT equipment is no longer restricted to a single location or even a few different remote sites. Cloud environments are still being used by businesses to run some, if not all, of their operations. Malware Let's take a look at some of the threats that can affect enterprise environments, starting with malware. The term malware is derived from combining the words "malicious software" into one word, and it is a broad term that encompasses a wide range of threats. To name a few, threats include viruses, Trojans, backdoors, worms, rootkits, spyware, exploits, adware, and any potentially unwanted programs.

Types of Malware

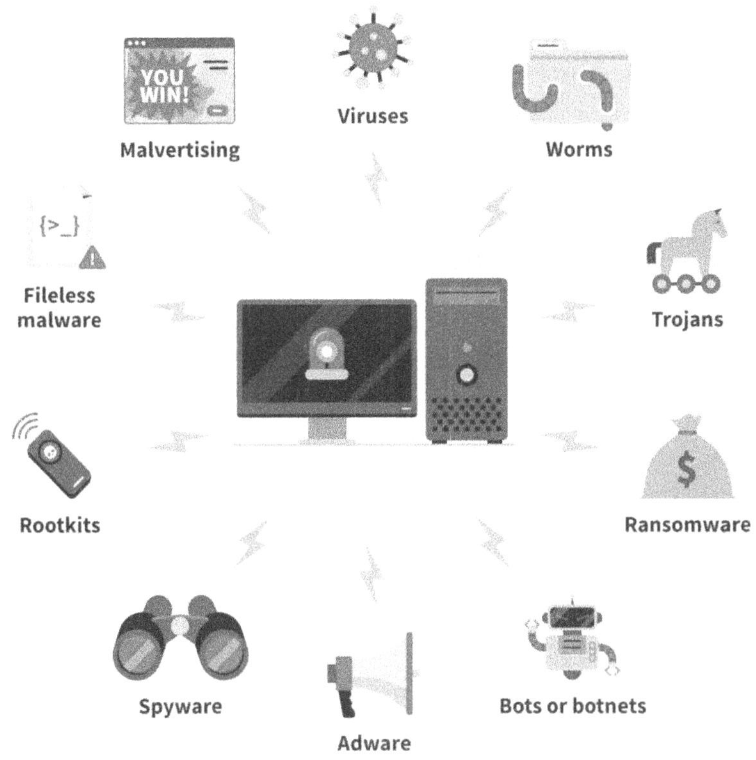

Virus Viruses are one of the oldest types of malware. While some people confuse malware and viruses, the most accurate definition of a virus is a computer program that copies itself. The virus spreads from one file to the next, eventually infecting enough files to cause serious computer damage. Although a single infected file can cause damage, viruses can also spread from computer to computer when infected files are transferred via a shared drive, USB drive, or any other medium of the file transfer. A virus is a piece of executable code that attaches itself to another program, such as an executable file or a macro within a Microsoft Office file.

The virus remains dormant until the infected file is executed, at which point the virus's code is executed. The virus's primary goal is to cause havoc. It accomplishes this by corrupting files, including system files, so that the underlying operating system does not function properly. Spyware Another type of malware is spyware. Spyware, as the name suggests, is designed to run on a victim's computer and steal sensitive information. Spyware can take the form of a key logger, which records each keystroke. If a victim visits a banking website and then logs in, the attacker will be able to see the keystrokes to determine which banking website the user was visiting, as well as the username and password. Spyware can also find credit card numbers, browsing habits, and pretty much anything else that a victim does on the computer.

CHAPTER 10

TROJAN & RANSOMWARE

A trojan is another type of malware that is designed to cause serious harm. Trojans frequently do not appear to be malicious software, but they, like any other malware, contain code that is designed to perform a specific task. Trojans, unlike viruses, cannot replicate themselves. They must be set up by the user. A backdoor Trojan is a common type of Trojan that is designed to give the attacker access to the infected computer, allowing them to do whatever they want with it. They can add the lead, or even send and receive various files, or perhaps the Trojan's sole purpose is to annoy the user by displaying AD pop-ups or simply changing the desktop background. The attacker can also take control of multiple machines and use them to attack other victims. In a Distributed Denial of Service attack, the attacker can have all infected computers attempt to bring down a system. In the following chapter, we will discuss Denial of Service and Distributed Denial of Service attacks.

38

Ransomware A specific type of Trojan is designed to infect a user's computer and render it inoperable. The only way for the victim to gain access to their computer and files is to pay the attacker a fee. This type of Trojan is known as ransomware because the attacker demands that the victim pay a ransom.

CHAPTER 11

ROOTKITS & WORMS

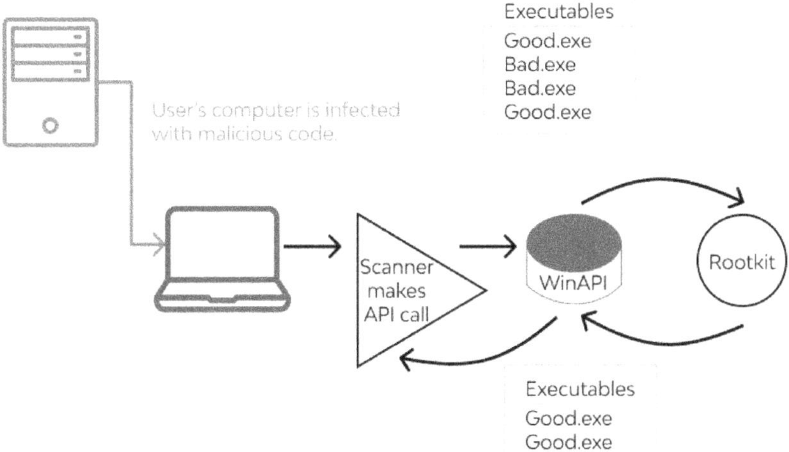

Rootkits are another type of malware.

RootKits are designed to perform many of the same malicious actions as some of the other malware we've discussed. The most significant distinction is that rootkits are specifically designed to avoid detection by traditional antimalware software.

They can accomplish this by inserting themselves into the computer's kernel, which is the same level as the host operating system. This gives attackers complete control of the computer, including the ability to overwrite or delete operating system files.

Worms

Worms are a type of malware that is distinct from viruses.

They replicate themselves in the same way that viruses do, but they are not attached to another program and do not require the user or host program to help spread the worm.

Worms exploit a vulnerability in the target system in order to spread from system to system. This is why it is critical to keep operating systems and software up to date.

Adware

Another type of malware is adware, which generates revenue by displaying advertisements on an infected machine. The malware's creator earns money by displaying advertisements or using a pay-per-click model.

Malware will almost certainly evolve alongside computer and network systems as they continue to evolve. This is why it is more important than ever to ensure that you, as a security engineer, are up to date on the various types of threats that exist, as well as how to mitigate them.

CHAPTER 12

DOS ATTACKS

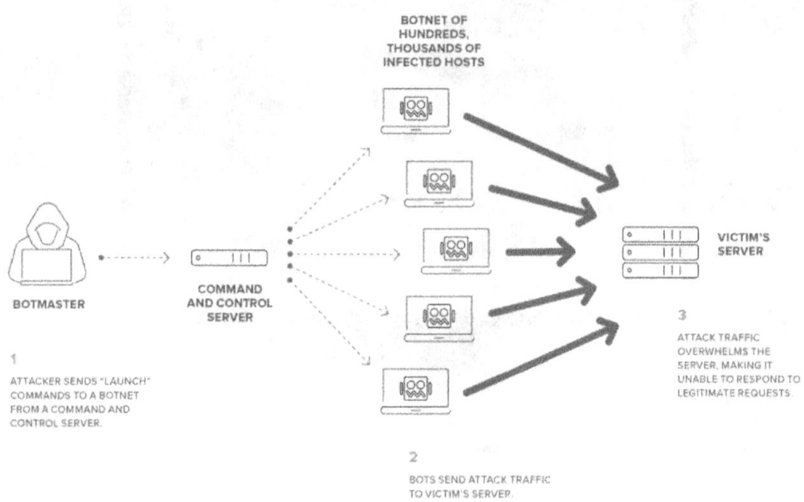

Numerous threats are not specifically malware.

We will discuss Denial of Service and Distributed Denial of Service attacks, as well as man-in-the-middle attacks, in this chapter.

Denial of Service (DoS) attack

A Denial of Service (DoS) attack occurs when a system's services are rendered inoperable to legitimate users. A system could be a web server, an email server, or any other service that is dependent on a computer or a network of computers.

A malicious attacker must send so much traffic that the service's server does not have enough resources to respond to every piece of traffic to effectively orchestrate a DoS attack.

This could be accomplished by sending a large number of ICMP messages, messages that attempt to initiate but never complete the three-way handshake, UDP messages, or any other type of message that the service is designed to respond to under normal conditions.

When a system or service becomes overburdened, it is unable to process any incoming legitimate requests, and users are denied access to the service.

Attack on Distributed Denial of Service (DDoS)

A Distributed Denial of Service (DDoS) attack occurs when multiple machines collaborate to attack a service.

The attacker can command malware-infected machines to send various types of messages to the intended victim of the DDoS attack.

CHAPTER 13

MAN-IN-THE-MIDDLE ATTACKS

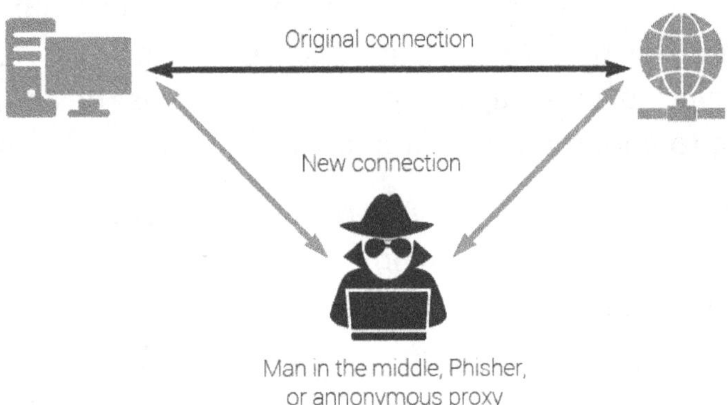

When someone intercepts traffic between two otherwise normal systems, this is referred to as a man-in-the-middle attack. For example, if a malicious attacker intercepted traffic between a client and a server, they would be able to see the entire contents of the traffic. A man-in-the-middle attack intercepts the client's initial request to the server, then copies that message and sends it to the original server. The server then responds to the man-in-the-middle with its return message. Once again, the man-in-the-middle copies the traffic and then replies to the client with the copy. The man-in-the-middle can repeat this process throughout the entire conversation between the client and the server. Both the client and the server believe they are conversing with each other, unaware that there is a device in the middle that can see the entire conversation. Furthermore, a man-in-the-middle attacker with the right tools could inject whatever they wanted into the communication between the client and the server. So they can not only read the contents of the conversation but also manipulate it in any way they want. The threats discussed in previous chapters, such as SQL injection and cross-site scripting, can also be used to wreak havoc on devices located both on-premises and in the cloud.

CHAPTER 14

SOCIAL ENGINEERING AND PHISHING ATTACKS

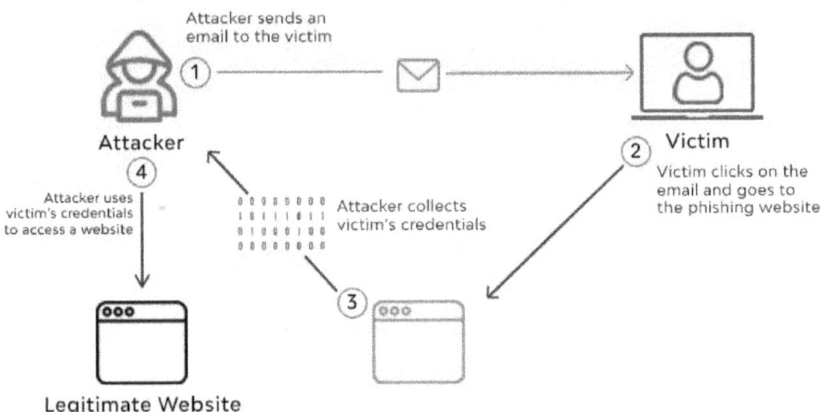

Another type of attack that has been on the rise in recent years is known as a social engineering attack. When there is a perceived trust between the attacker and another party, this is an example of social engineering. The party could be the victim or a third-party, such as an internet service provider or email provider. Also, if the attacker can gain the provider's trust and persuade them that they are the victim's identity, the service provider may reveal confidential information that should only be disclosed to the victim, such as an account name and password. Once the attacker has this information, they can use it to obtain additional information or even change the service to prevent the victim from using it. If the attacker has completed social engineering attacks directly with the victim, they are convincing the victim that they are a trusted authority. There are several methods that attackers can use to gather enough information to gain the victim's trust. In today's world, using social media and other online profiles of the victim is a common method. Regardless of the method used to collect information, once trust is established, the attacker can use it to persuade the victim that all correspondence is legitimate. This means they can send emails with malicious links. If the user believes the email is legitimate, they are much more likely to click on the link.

The email does not even have to contain a malicious file. Assume the attacker learned that the victim was buying a house and needed to send a large wire transfer for the down payment. Normally, the funds are transferred to a title company. If the attacker uses social engineering to convince the victim that they are the title company, they may provide an incorrect banking number, causing the victim to send money to the attacker rather than the legitimate title company. Bulk Phishing Phishing is a common method for launching a social engineering attack. Phishing is the use of electronic communications to gain the trust of an unsuspecting user.

There are several types of phishing. Bulk phishing occurs when no specific individual or organization is targeted; instead, the attacker will launch a phishing campaign and target as many people as possible to gain as many victims as possible who fall for the phishing attempt. Phishing is a type of fraud. When an attacker attempts to target a specific individual or organization, this is referred to as spear phishing. To increase their chances of success, the attacker will conduct research and gather as much information about their intended target as possible. The earlier example of the attacker impersonating a title company is an example of a spear-phishing attack. The attacker was aware that the victim was planning to purchase a home and was most likely aware of the title company that the victim intended to use. Again, having this information gave the attacker a better chance of success because they would know information that the victim believes only a legitimate person or company would know. Whaling Whaling is a subset of spear phishing that attempts to target senior executives and other high-profile targets. The content used by the attacker to gain the victim's trust would be tailored to target upper management. clone Phishing

A clone phishing attack occurs when an attacker duplicates an otherwise legitimate service or company to impersonate them.

Continuing with our impersonation of the title company, the attacker may have made a copy of a legitimate wire transfer form and then edited it to look almost identical except the updated router number.

If the attacker sends the victim the new form and then calls the victim to say they made a mistake on the original document and should use the one provided by the attacker, this is an example of clone phishing.

As I mentioned earlier, phishing attempts use a variety of techniques to trick their victims into clicking on malicious content. For example, link manipulation is commonly used to make links appear to go to a legitimate organization but go to a malicious site or destination.

Sometimes the domain link contains misspellings of the website that the attacker is pretending to represent. Another example would be to create a website with a legitimate-looking subdomain.

For example, some users may believe that the site will take the victim to the title company's updated wire transfer section. When, in reality, it takes them to the title company's subdomain of the updated wire transfer website, where the attacker owns both the fake wire transfer site and the title company subdomain. This means that any information provided to the title company's subdomain can be retrieved by the attacker.

Website forgery

Phishing attacks can also make use of website forgery. This involves using JavaScript to make the address bar look like the website the attacker is attempting to impersonate. If the address bar displays the correct URL of the website that the attacker was attempting to impersonate, the user will have a difficult time determining that they are going to the wrong website.

CHAPTER 15

MITIGATE PHISHING ATTACKS

We've talked about social engineering attacks, which include phishing, so let's talk about different ways to mitigate phishing. One of the most effective ways to reduce phishing attempts is to train the user base by preparing them to recognize common tactics used by phishing attackers. As a result, if they see any of these techniques, they are less likely to click on malicious links or attachments in an email. Here are some helpful hints for teaching your user base. First, you should have them double-check that the domain name looks correct before clicking on any of the links, regardless of who is sending them. Another suggestion is for users to ask themselves if the email makes complete sense.

As an example, imagine attacking a corporate user in finance and including a link to an invoice. If the user attempts to inquire whether it makes sense that they are receiving the invoice, this will help raise red flags. Perhaps they are expecting an invoice, but the "from address" appears to be unfamiliar. This brings me to my next point. If the phishing attempt appears plausible, instruct the user to call to confirm. Even if the attacker was able to spoof the "from address" to be the correct domain or even an email address, the user should call to confirm that an invoice was sent. If a phishing attempt is detected, do not have the user respond; instead, train the user to mark the email as spam to help prevent further phishing attempts from passing through the company's filters. Finally, teach users that if they happen to click on a malicious link, they should immediately contact their IT department or security team.

This will aid in minimizing the damage as soon as possible. There are services available that allow you to simulate a phishing attempt by running campaigns against your user base. There are no malicious links included; instead, the link redirects the user to a Landing Page with even more useful tips on what to look for. However, even though user training is very effective, it is not always sufficient. As we've seen in previous chapters, phishing attacks are becoming increasingly sophisticated. If an attacker devises a new method that the userbase has not been trained on, the user is more likely to fall for the phishing attempt. This is where technology enters the picture. There are much-advanced phishing protection exists that analyzes emails that make it through the initial secure email gateway, then it analyzes these emails using various methods such as advanced machine learning techniques, relationship modeling, real-time behavior analytics, as well as telemetry to quickly identify if the email is a phishing attempt or not. If the email is determined to be a phishing attempt or malicious, the advanced phishing protection can be configured to have the emails discarded or even redirected to be further analyzed.

This can be done in-house or with a security partner like Cisco. Cisco security experts will assist your organization in fully comprehending the consequences of various phishing and social engineering attempts. By implementing technology to assist with phishing, any new phishing technique discovered elsewhere can be used to protect the organization. This means that along with training the users on how to spot malicious attempts, your organization can be confident that anything they are not being trained on has a reduced likelihood that the phishing attempt will be successful.

CHAPTER 16

CLOUD SERVICES ATTACKS

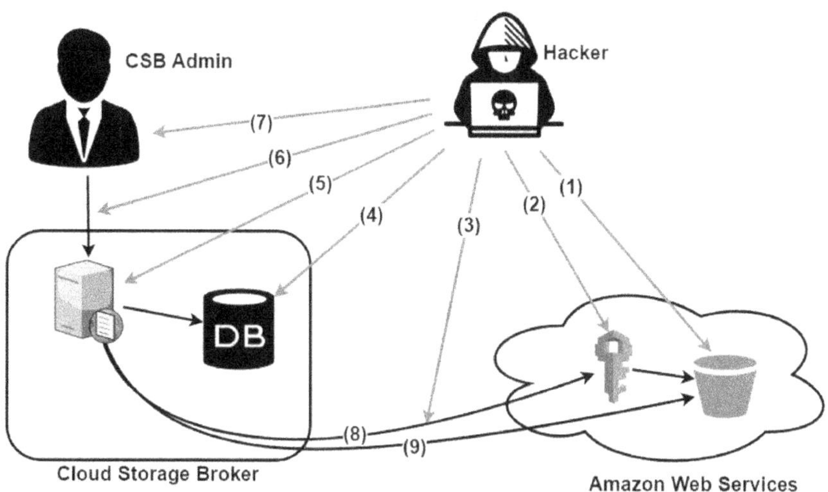

While all of the attacks mentioned thus far can affect devices hosted in a cloud environment, I want to focus on specific threats that can occur against cloud environments in this chapter. There are a few non-profit organizations that provide guidelines for security engineers to ensure the security of their systems.

The cloud security alliance, or CSA, is one of them, and as the name implies, they are concerned with cloud security. The Open Web Application Security Project, or OWASP, is dedicated to developing secure web applications and keeps a top ten list of vulnerabilities. Breach of cloud data The first cloud-related threat I'd like to discuss with you is a cloud data breach. A data breach occurs when an attacker gains access to information that should be kept private by hacking into the system where the information is stored. As more organizations choose to store their data in the cloud, that data becomes more vulnerable if any of the security measures are not properly configured. When an attacker identifies a system with low security, it becomes much easier for them to gain access to that system.

According to the CSA, a lack of security could be caused by human error, application vulnerabilities, or simply poor security practices in general. Once the attackers gain access to the system, they have access to all of the files stored on it. Application programming interfaces, or APIs, are used to take advantage of the many benefits that cloud computing provides. APIs enable connections and authorized data sharing to take place automatically. Still, as with the previous threats we've discussed, APIs that aren't secure are vulnerable to attack, threats like creating an API request with an embedded threat or obtaining API keys and using them to impersonate a legitimate application attempting to make an API request. If the API does not follow the principle of least privilege, this is another security concern that would allow a threat actor to do even more damage than if the API did. API gateways can be used to have all API connections terminate at the same location.

API security gateways are recommended by the OWASP Foundation. API security gateways offer the same functionality as API gateways, but as the name implies, they include security technologies. When the API gateways were designed, security was not a top priority; rather, functionality was. As a result, they are vulnerable to an attacker gaining access. Account management is another issue for cloud systems. Similar to organizations that host our systems on-premise, if admin accounts are not properly managed and passwords are not properly changed when an administrator leaves an organization, this poses an additional security risk. Operators are vulnerable to attack if the organization does not properly manage and authenticate them. Using multifactor authentication is a good way to protect against stolen credentials. Denial of Service and Distributed Denial of Service attacks are a risk for cloud-hosted systems, just as they are for on-premise systems.

CHAPTER 17

SECURITY INTELLIGENCE BASICS

We have already learned about various threats that can affect both on-premises and cloud-hosted environments. We also discussed social engineering and phishing attacks, so in the following chapters, we will discuss security intelligence fundamentals. First, we'll go over a quick overview of what security intelligence is, and then you'll learn about the various components that make security intelligence so effective. Finally, you will learn about Cisco Talos, which is Cisco's solution for security intelligence. As we've seen in previous chapters, numerous threats can impact an enterprise network. As time goes on, it is almost certain that new types of attacks will emerge that do not exist today.

The days of network security engineers simply configuring a firewall to block specific ports and IP addresses and then sitting back to monitor are long gone. As a security engineer, you must ensure the security of your network daily, as new threats emerge. In today's ever-changing security landscape, it would be nearly impossible for a department of dedicated security engineers to ensure that all of their devices are updated with the most up-to-date rule sets to keep the organization safe. With so many different entry points for threats into the network, the job becomes exponentially more difficult. Emails, corporate laptops, BYOD, malicious websites, and devices in the DMZ are just a few examples of the various points of entry that threats have to enter the network.

A team of security engineers would have to conduct extensive research just to identify the most recent threats. Once identified, they must determine the best way to mitigate against them. After that, they would have to implement the changes, and if the threat was rising quickly, it is quite possible that your company would be compromised by the threat before the security team had time to research to see what new threats were out there. Investigate ways to mitigate the threat, and then put the changes into action. This is where security intelligence comes in. Security intelligence enables organizations to join a larger community of network security devices.

The community benefits as a whole as a result of this. If a security intelligence organization anywhere in the world encounters a previously unseen threat, there is now information on it. While that organization may have been compromised, the information gathered and shared will allow all other organizations to better protect themselves from it. There are various security intelligence clouds out there that all revolve around the same concepts, but they must first author the security intelligence. Once the intelligence is created, the cloud must distribute it to the participants. Finally, each member must consume the intelligence and apply it in a way that makes sense. In the following chapter, I'll go over the various aspects of security intelligence.

CHAPTER 18

AUTHORING THE INTELLIGENCE

First, let's talk about who created the intelligence. To author any intelligence about the current threats, information must first be provided. Telemetry sharing is a very powerful way for the security intelligence cloud to discover what is happening in real-time to an organization's networks. Telemetry sharing occurs when the devices themselves upload the data that they have seen to a larger network or cloud for further analysis. Continue with the previous chapter's example of a global organization that encountered a previously unseen threat. Let's call that organization Sunshine Store. When a threat affects Sunshine Store, their devices now have valuable information about that threat. If they participate in threat telemetry sharing, this information is shared with the rest of the security intelligence cloud. This is done automatically from the device to the cloud and does not require any manual intervention from the security engineer. Every other organization in the security intelligence cloud is also sharing critical information about cloud threats. All of the sharing provides valuable context about the threat that could not have come from a single source. Perhaps the threat occurs at the same time of day for each organization, or perhaps the threat is limited to a specific country or industry. Better inferences can be made by having a larger sample pool contribute data to the cloud.

A cloud will then perform various tasks on the information, such as normalizing it and analyzing it to find patterns. The intelligence clouds can determine various factors such as the type of threat, the frequency with which the attack occurs, the surface area within the organization that the threat used to gain access to, the severity of the impact, and many more metrics. As previously stated, when the cloud analyses threats, it determines whether there are targeted industries, targeted nations, or other patterns. As more information about the threat becomes available, the security intelligence cloud can devise various countermeasures. The security intelligence cloud can now generate different signatures and content updates for all of the cloud's products.

The organization's email security devices will participate in the security intelligence cloud, and an update will be issued to that email secure device for it to block the threat. For example, if another company decided to join the threat intelligence cloud, such as Cisco Talos, they would provide the email security appliance with the most recent updates to block threats identified as using email as the attack medium. This is the same as an intrusion prevention system. An update would be created around all threats that can be stopped using an IPS, or Intrusion Prevention System. As a result, any IPS that install that update will block this new threat. Cisco Talos would receive an update on the company's next-generation intrusion prevention system. This leads us to the sharing and consumption of security intelligence. Now that the security intelligence cloud has created various updates and signatures for the threats that it has encountered, it is time to share them with the rest of the security intelligence community.

This is typically accomplished through the use of content update pushes, and organizations such as Cisco Talos have content updates every 3-5 minutes. Once the update has been downloaded, each device must now install it, and once the content has been installed, each device is now ready to block the latest threat. Similarly, a new threat has affected organizations within the security intelligence cloud, including Sunshine Store. Because another company was participating in the cloud, as soon as the threat was analyzed, the appropriate mitigations were discovered and the updates were created, pushed, and installed. This new company is now safe from this new threat. What makes this so beneficial is that it occurs without any manual intervention from the security engineer.

They no longer need to conduct this research on their own, figure out how to stop it, and then manually apply their changes. Speaking of research, I'd like to point out that security intelligence information sharing does not only refer to the automatic updates that devices receive. It is an entire ecosystem that enables security professionals to understand the threats as well. While it is great that network security devices can be automatically configured to stop new threats, it would be a disservice if administrators were unaware of the threats and mitigations that were being implemented.

Having a better understanding of the most recent security threats will only benefit you as a security engineer. The more you are aware of the various types of threats and the actual methods they use to infiltrate networks and cause havoc, the better you will be able to understand the big picture.

CHAPTER 19

ARP POISONING

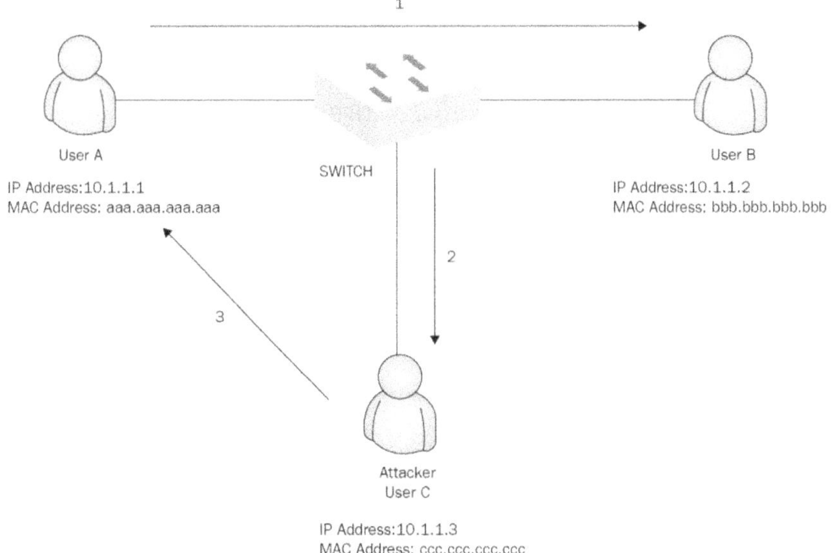

When it comes to a Man in the Middle attack, it can take many forms, but the most common is known as ARP poisoning.

To understand ARP poisoning, you must first understand how ARP, also known as Address Resolution Protocol, works.

ARP converts IP addresses to MAC addresses, also known as physical addresses, of all networking devices connected to a specific network device. The command on a Windows machine is "arp –a," but the same command can be used on other operating systems as well.

To launch Command Prompt on a Windows operating system, click the Start button, type Command Prompt, and press Enter. After that, simply type arp and press enter to see all options related to the arp command.

After you've done that, you'll notice the following variations;

• Arp – a > This command displays the current ARP entries connected to the network that the computer is aware of, listing both the IP and MAC addresses of those devices.

• Arp – d > This command removes the ARP entry for the host you specify.

• Arp – s > This command will assist you in adding hosts and assigning them an IP address.

• Arp – v > This command displays the current ARP entries in verbose mode, as well as all invalid entries and the loopback interface.

These are some of the basic variations and options available when it comes to ARP, but it is not necessary to be aware of all available options.

To return to ARP poisoning, once connected, computers and networking devices on the same network learn each other's Mac Addresses. They will create an ARP table once they have learned each other's MAC addresses, and they will use that table to locate each other on the same network in the future.

This is how ARP assists computers and networking devices in easily discovering each other on the network; however, hackers would take advantage of ARP tables by introducing themselves on the network with bogus MAC addresses, fooling computers into thinking they were the new Router. As a result, the real ARP table would be tainted with bogus entries.

Once the Man in the Middle has poisoned the ARP table, the computer will believe that the new route to the internet is the new IP Address. As a result, every packet sent to the internet would be routed through the attacker.

There are numerous ways to accomplish this using both wired and wireless networks. ARP poisoning via Man in the Middle attack can be accomplished in a variety of ways, but the concepts are always the same.

CHAPTER 20

ROGUE ACCESS POINTS

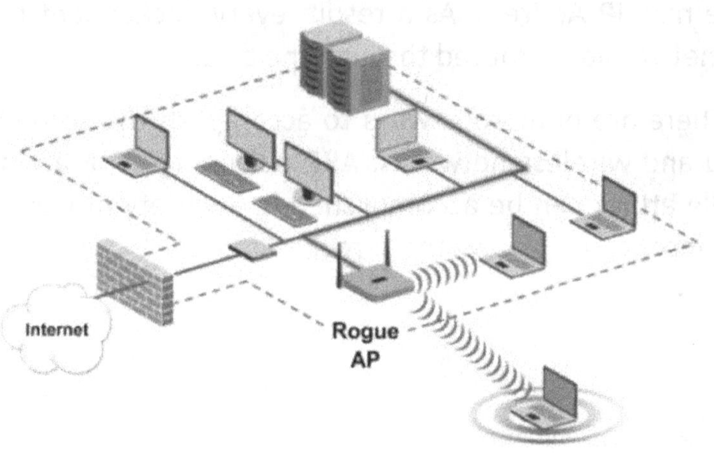

There are numerous ways to attack wireless networks, but let's start with the fundamentals. Most people want to use free WiFi wherever they can; in fact, there are free wireless networks in many public places these days.

Wireless networks are becoming more prevalent as more Access Points are deployed, sending wireless signals over the internet.

Chatting on mobile devices, voice calls, live streaming, Internet banking, shopping, and other activities are examples of these signals.

Because wireless networks are so prevalent in our daily lives, hackers have begun to exploit them by employing various techniques to gain control of Wireless Networks.

Previously, hackers used wireless networks to gain access to company networks. Despite the fact that wireless networks are more secure, hackers continue to gain access through Wireless Access Points because many organizations do not implement good security measures within their Wireless Networks.

People like to use free WIFI Hotspots, as I mentioned earlier, but many of us are unaware of the dangers of connecting to a Rogue Access Point that advertises itself as a genuine Free WIFI Hotspot.

It is very simple to set up a rogue access point; therefore, large organizations must have a variety of security measures in place to protect their Wireless Network.

Most access points do not use electricity; instead, they are PoE devices that use Power over Ethernet. As a result, access points must be linked to another network device that is turned on, such as a network switch. Because access points are not small, you will not see hackers walking around with one in their hands.

Instead, hackers can use an operating system like Kali Linux to virtualize Access Points within a laptop. Hacking wireless networks are simple once Kali Linux is installed and bridged on a laptop.

To become a Rogue Access Point on a Wireless Network, configure Kali Linux to begin monitoring Wireless signals and then analyze existing genuine Access Points in greater detail. Following that, you can learn the MAC addresses of the valid access points as well as the channel they use to transmit wireless signals.

With that information, you can configure Kali Linux to advertise the same information as the valid Access Point, and then become the new fake Access Point, also known as a Rogue Access Point.

There are many other configurations required, such as DHCP services or DHCP Server settings, to provide IP addresses to the clients who are now also victims, but Kali Linux makes the job very easy for any unskilled person as well.

Another setting required for Rogue Access Points is "NAT," or Network Address Translation, which converts private IP addresses to public IP addresses. Finally, routing functionality must be configured so that victims can communicate with the internet via the Rogue Access Point.

Rogue Access Points are also known as Man in the Middle attacks because they are placed between the victim and the destination address that the victim is visiting.

CHAPTER 21

MAN IN THE MIDDLE ON WIRELESS NETWORKS

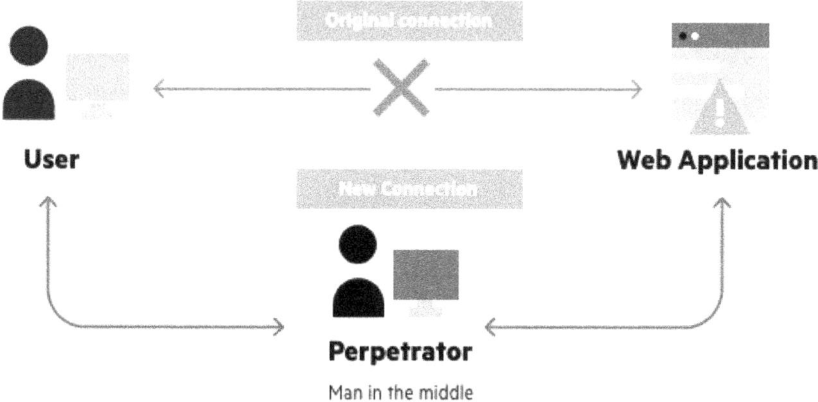

To continue, once there is a Man in the Middle, the Man in the Middle can capture anything the end-user does, including any website visits where usernames or passwords are required to be typed.

In addition to capturing data, a Man in the Middle can modify details or even change data entry that the victim provides, such as when filling out important online forms. One of the most common ways that the Man in the Middle attack is used is to have victims connect to a Rogue Access Point via wireless networks.

This is critical to understand, and end-users must be trained to always verify the Wireless SSID to which they are connecting.

69

Attacks Based on Misconceptions

You can use operating systems like Kali Linux to replicate or create any MAC address, allowing your laptop to function as any other network device.

As a result, once you start monitoring wireless signals with your Virtualized Kali Linux, you can begin identifying Wireless Networks, where you can identify both the Access Point and the Clients that are associated with the Access Points.

Once you have those details, you can either fake the MAC address of the Access Point and become a Rogue Wireless Access Point, or you can learn enough about the connected clients to begin replicating them.

The MAC addresses of successfully connected devices are learned and remembered by most access points. That's why you don't have to type the password every time you connect to a wireless network to which you've previously provided a password.

You won't even have to click or select the SSID again because your device will automatically connect to trusted access points while in your pocket. However, keep in mind that trust between the client and the Access Point must be mutual. So the client device must not only trust the Wireless Access Point, but the Wireless Access Point must also trust the client device.

Once Kali Linux has discovered the MAC address of an existing Client that has already established a connection with a trusted Wireless Access Point, all you have to do is replicate the trusted device's MAC address and assign it to your own Kali Linux Wireless Interface.

By replicating a trusted Client's Mac Address and assigning it to your own Kali Linux interface, you still need to figure out how to connect to the wireless network, and this is where the trick comes in. To de-authenticate all existing trusted connected clients, send a de-authentication message to the Access Point.

While all previously trusted clients would attempt to re-authenticate themselves to the wireless network to gain internet access, your device must connect to the wireless access point faster than the previously trusted device. You can use Kali Linux to make your wireless signal stronger to connect to the wireless access point faster.

CHAPTER 22

DE-AUTHENTICATION ATTACK

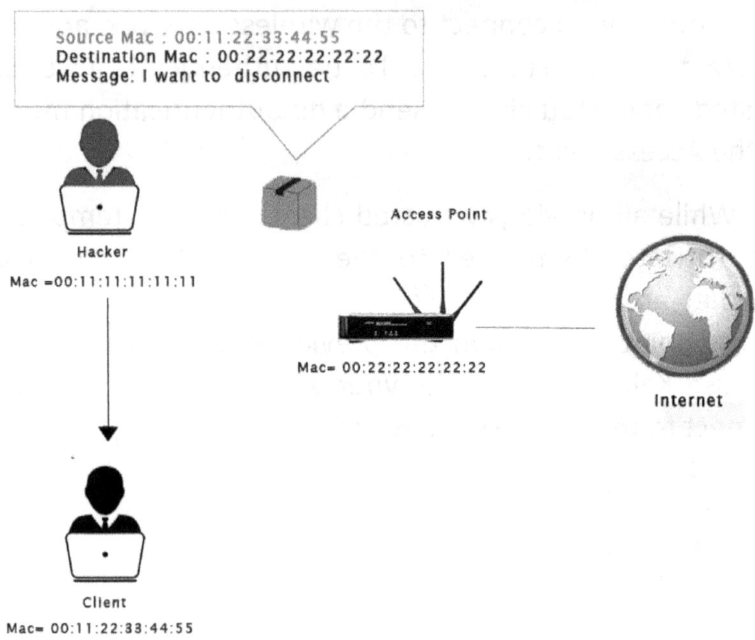

The goal of a Mis-Association Attack is for a hacker to become authenticated and authorized on a wireless network. Once you connect to a wireless network, you can do a variety of things, and hackers don't use this technique for the sole purpose of obtaining free wireless internet, but rather to carry out a more sophisticated attack.

The most common reason for hacking is for financial gain, but there are other reasons for hacking as well, such as espionage or impersonation.

Sometimes hackers only intend to cause a simple network delay, something that would slow down the network, or cause issues such as individual devices failing to operate properly or connect to the network.

With a tool like Kali Linux, you can monitor and learn all MAC addresses of trusted clients that are connected to the network, and once you've learned enough data about the clients, you can run an automated de-authentication request for every single trusted device that originates from an attacking laptop.

The attacking laptop or Kali Linux would appear to the AP aka Access Point as if all re-authentication requests were coming from existing clients. In turn, the AP would deauthenticate all of those devices, leaving end-users perplexed as to why they had lost Internet access.

Once reported to the IT Department, engineers should have enough time to analyze the logs and figure out what happened, but they won't find anything other than normal traffic flow. However, if everyone disconnects from the same wireless network at the same or similar time, this raises suspicion. Still, it would be difficult to determine what exactly occurred and where the traffic initiation of several de-authentication requests originated.

CHAPTER 23

WIRELESS COLLISION ATTACK

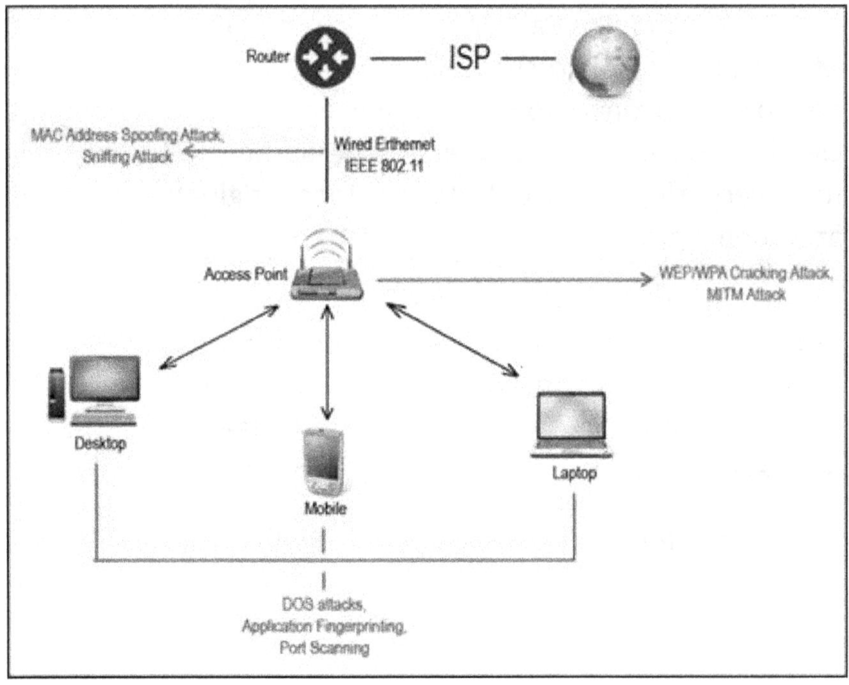

Wireless collisions are common and can be unintentionally caused by devices such as cordless phones and microwaves that cause interference, weakening wireless signals for existing trusted connected devices.

Wireless access points use various channels to send signals through the air. For example, if you live in a flat, your neighbor's wireless access point may cause wireless interference to your home connection.

Access points have a signal range of 30-50 meters, but some Ap-s designed for enterprise use can transmit wireless signals up to 600 meters if there is no interference and no obstruction within reach.

When wireless signals encounter obstacles such as windows, doors, walls, and thicker objects, their quality begins to deteriorate. Weak wireless signals are common in flats, especially if you have multiple neighbors leaving nearby.

I already mentioned that you can configure Kali Linux to provide stronger wireless signals, as well as monitor and identify wireless SSIDs, wireless access points in range, and the channel on which they operate.

Hackers frequently configure their Kali Linux to use the same channels as the victims' AP-s, causing significant wireless interference, causing the victim's network to become not only slow but in some cases completely useless.

By continuously increasing wireless signals, packets would eventually be dropped, and most, if not all, clients would be unable to connect to the wireless network. Taking this a step further, hackers install Kali on a Raspberry Pi and hide it near the targeted wireless access point to cause even worse wireless signals.

In some cases, hackers attach a Raspberry Pi pre-configured to run Kali Linux to a Drone and land it on the targeted building. When a sophisticated wireless collision attack is used, wireless signals can be severely weakened, affecting multiple SSIDs and even multiple APs. Clients would drop off the wireless network as a result of Wireless Collision Attacks.

CHAPTER 24

WIRELESS REPLAY ATTACKS

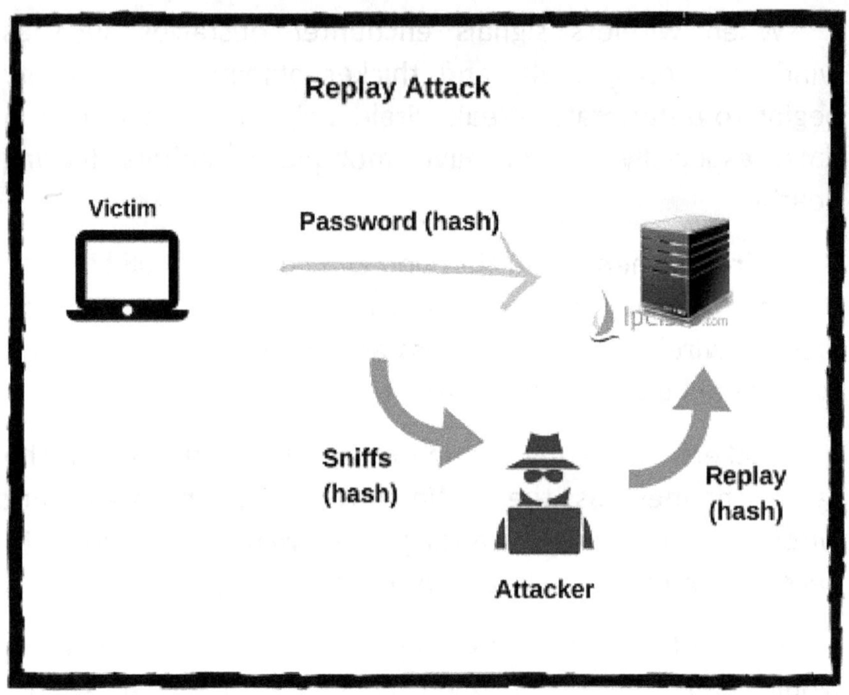

Wireless Replay attacks have fallen out of favor, but they were once very common. At the same time, wireless replay attacks continue to be used on wireless networks for a variety of reasons.

Capturing wireless signals is simple, especially since they are all around us. Before connecting to a wireless network, a hacker must first monitor the wireless signals.

Wireshark software can be used to record wireless traffic while monitoring it. Wireshark is packet analysis software that network engineers frequently use to troubleshoot wired and wireless network issues.

Wireshark can assist in further analyzing captured traffic and understanding what type of communication is taking place on the wireless network. A hacker would specifically examine packets associated with the client authentication process to a specific SSID.

This packet would validate the password used to connect to the wireless access point. Once the hacker has access to the data, he can use it to send the same message over the air to the AP. As a result, the access point would authenticate and authorize the hacker to connect to the network on the assumption that it is a known trusted device.

Because most large corporations are already implementing new security practices for better encryption, Wireless Replay attacks are not as common as they once were. However, not all organizations use strong encryption techniques, and many businesses could be exploited by employing this antiquated method.

CHAPTER 25

PROTECTING WIRELESS NETWORKS

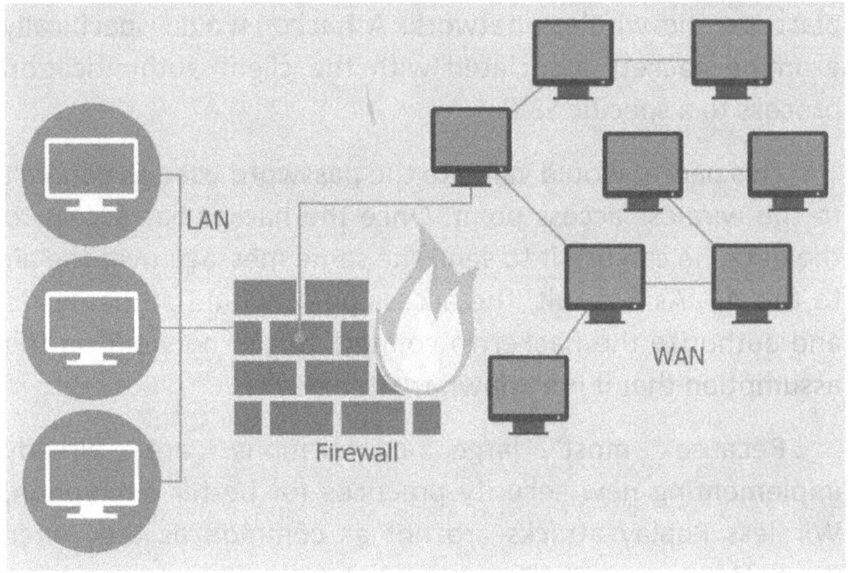

Because infrastructure security is critical, most large companies already have good security in places, such as Cisco Identity Service Engine (ISE), Cisco, Checkpoint, or Palo Alto Firewalls, and some sort of Intrusion Prevention System (APS) and Intrusion Detection System (IDS) such as Cisco FirePower.

Most businesses prefer to have two types of firewalls, just in case one of them is compromised.

Intrusion Detection Systems are also well-known for wireless security and are excellent at detecting network anomalies. Engineers and security professionals will be notified via e-mail once anomalies are discovered. One thing to keep in mind is that IDS-s are only very good at identifying or detecting anomalies, not stopping them.

This is where Intrusion Prevention Systems come in, as they can prevent or mitigate such wireless attacks. The issue with intrusion detection systems is that, while they are effective at preventing hacks, they are not very effective at detecting them. As a result, having both devices and virtual appliances IPS-s and IDS-s is a good practice.

The majority of Wireless Access Points are Power over Ethernet devices and thus are connected to network switches. Additional commands must be implemented on network switches if a hacker attempts to connect to the network via wired or wireless connections.

Wireless network security is critical, and if you have a personal wireless network at home, you are most likely using a protocol like WPA-Personal or WPA-PSK. PSK is an abbreviation for Pre-shared Key, which is a password required to connect to a wireless network.

A pre-shared key can be compromised using a variety of techniques, including a brute-force attack or a dictionary attack. Brute-force and dictionary attacks are both relatively simple tasks to carry out, especially with Kali Linux.

Running these tools requires only a few clicks, and once started, they will begin the job of locating the password or Pre-shared Key.

Pre-shared keys should contain both uppercase and lowercase letters, numbers, and various symbols, as well as at least 12 characters. The more complex your password, the more difficult it is for a hacker to crack.

Furthermore, your password should not be associated with you. Please refrain from using your name, date of birth, or any names that belong to family members.

Most people use passwords that are simple to remember. Of course, the bad guys are aware of this, and by using social networking sites, they can easily crack passwords related to individuals.

Brute-force or dictionary attacks can crack passwords, and even if it takes days, they will eventually be broken. This is one of the primary reasons why companies implement password policies such as password complexity and requiring users to change passwords regularly. These are standard practices, and if they have not yet been implemented in your organization, you should bring them to the attention of your manager.

BONUS CHAPTER VPN CONCEPTS

What do you consider a VPN to be? If I said to you, "Hey, we're setting up a VPN," what would you think or how would you define it? So, here's how some of us have defined it.

First and foremost, VPN stands for Virtual Private Networking. Let's get back to the virtual part of things. Let us instead begin with private networking.

Private networking implies that I can network and send data and other such things while remaining private, correct? There's an assumption that whatever I send over the network is private to me, so the virtual part comes in here: my network is private, but it's a virtual network.

VPNs are what we call an overlay technology because they sit on top of another network that already exists. We're putting our virtual private network on top of an existing network or a collection of networks that we'll be traversing.

So that's how a virtual private network is envisioned. What services do VPNs provide, and why are they so important? As an overlay, a VPN is typically designed to connect remote sites or users in remote locations over a wide area network.

We could do it via public network access such as the internet, or we could do VPNs over private wide area networks. But the idea is that it connects us across multiple sites, and because we're sending traffic over a public network that we don't control, the VPN should provide some level of confidentiality for us and our data. So that will take the form of encryption.

There are several encryption technologies that we could use, and you may be familiar with some of them already. So, many years ago, the most popular encryption technology was DES or Data Encryption Standard. There was 3DES, which was three distinct DES processes.

These are still in use, and some organizations do, but DES and 3DES are considered to be older protocols. Instead, we'd employ the Advanced Encryption Standard (AES).

DES is a 56-bit encryption algorithm. 3DES is 168 bits, and AES can be 128 bits, 168 bits, 256 bits, and so on. There are various AES groups, encryption methods, and strengths that we can employ.

As a result, we would select these based on the level of encryption required, which is the level of confidentiality. So, if we wanted to be secure, AES-256 is probably a good choice.

VPN should also ensure data integrity, ensuring that data is not tampered with while in transit. Consider it this way:

Let's say we have a box and we're sending it from one location to another, so we put it on a scale and weigh it, and we say it weighs 20 pounds, and we send it off.

Someone messes with it while it's in transit. They open the box and take items from it. When the box reaches the other side of the line and is weighed, it weighs only two pounds.

We can look at the label and say, "Wait a minute, the shipping label said it was 20 pounds, but it only weighs 2 right now." This package's integrity has been compromised, so we don't open it, we don't tamper with it, we send it back, or we simply say, "Hey, I don't accept this." That is character.

We'll use a hash mechanism with VPNs to ensure data integrity. A hash algorithm can be used to create the hash mechanism. We have MD5, which is Message Digest 5, and SHA, which is a Secure Hash Algorithm, also known as SHA-1 or SHA-256 today.

So, essentially, we take the data packet and hash it, and then we attach the hash, just like weighing the box, and then we send it to the other side, and the other side will take the packet and hash it themselves.

So they'll run it through the hash algorithm, let's say SHA, and then they'll generate a hash, which is just some 3 or 5 hash, and they'll compare that hash to the hash that was sent. If the hash matches, we know it essentially weighs the same, and we're good to go, and we accept it. That's how VPNs help me maintain data integrity.

The third point we'll cover is that a VPN should provide me with data origin authentication. We can provide data origin authentication using a pre-shared key.

We'll simply use PSK, or pre-shared key, or a digital certificate, and the digital certificate would be similar to getting a driver's license from the DMV, so it's authenticated by a trusted third party.

For instance, if you go to the DMV and fill out your information, they will issue you a driver's license. If you are pulled over, you can show them your driver's license, and the police officer will trust it because it was issued by a trusted source, the DMV, and it authenticates you.

We can achieve the same result with a digital certificate. We can enroll with a CA server such as Verisign, Entrust, or GoDaddy, obtain a certificate, and then present that certificate to someone with whom we want to establish a VPN.

They can see who issued the certificate and thus trust them.

Because your certificate has been signed by them, I'm going to accept it. As a result, they can use certificates for origin authentication in this manner.

As an alternative, we can use a pre-shared key. So I take my data and, in essence, hash it with that pre-shared key before sending it to the other side. We shared that key with them as well; we did this offline, and they can compare the hashes; if they match, we'll talk.

These are the three things we want to understand about VPNs: confidentiality, data integrity, and data origin authentication. VPNs could also provide anti-replay protection, which they usually do. In terms of how that occurs, there isn't much to say.

It's built into the protocol, as well as iOS and Cisco ASA Firewalls, and they just do it, but these are the three pieces we'll have control over in our configuration. We've already discussed what causes a lot of this. We've discussed encryption protocols as well as hash algorithms. So far, we've discussed AES, 3DES, MD5, and SHA, but there's a little more to it, so let's go over some additional terminology.

First and foremost, consider how encryption keys are exchanged. There is, however, a protocol known as ISAKMP. The Internet Security Association Key Management Protocol is what it's called. We simply refer to it as ISAKMP, and many people refer to IKE, the Internet Key Exchange, which is a component of ISAKMP.

ISAKMP provides IKE, the Internet Key Exchange, and Oakley, and there are a few other protocols that sit beneath ISAKMP, but we just lump them all together. ISAKMP will negotiate a secure channel for us and exchange our keys in advance.

Those secure encryption keys could be generated using the Diffie-Hellman algorithm, abbreviated as DH. The Diffie-Hellman algorithm generates a secret key that is not exchanged across the wire, but in the end, we have these keys on both devices that they can use for encryption and decryption, symmetric keys, and we didn't send those keys across the wire, which is a good thing.

As a result, when we establish a connection, we create what is known as a security association. A security association is essentially an entry on my router that lists who I'm communicating with, what algorithms I'm using, and what keys I could use. So, before they can communicate with each other, both devices will have a SA or Security Association.

When we start sending packets, they will be formulated using either ESP, AH, or both, but in general, we will only use ESP these days. ESP stands for Encapsulating Security Payload, and we can use it in two modes: tunnel mode and transport mode. When we use ESP in tunnel mode, we have a private IP address that is tunneled inside of a public address.

So, that's a high-level overview of the ESP protocol. It is a protocol that is part of the IPsec protocol suite. If we look at the ESP header, we can see that it has a security parameter index number. It will have a security parameter index number, which will link it to a security association. We'll start with a sequence number, then the encrypted payload, some padding, and finally an integrity check.

The payload data contained within is the original IP packet that has been encrypted. We encrypt our data in tunnel mode and add an ESP header on top of it. That ESP header will provide me with information about the security parameter, index, and so on.

We'll add a new IP header that isn't encrypted and can be used to route traffic. While the ESP trailer should be encrypted, not all of it is because we wouldn't know where the end of the packet is if we didn't know where the end of the packet is, the majority of that trailer is encrypted and then we can authenticate this entire ESP header, plus the encrypted data and the ESP authentication, we can use SHA-1, SHA-256, or MD-5 to do the ESP authentication. That is if we are in tunnel mode.

When we're in transport mode, the data is encrypted but not the original IP header. So, if you tried to send private network traffic over the internet, you wouldn't be able to use transport mode because the IP header would be a private IP address rather than the public address. That is what the new header is for: to connect us to the internet. So that's what ESP is.

AH, on the other hand, is an abbreviation for Authentication Header. The authentication header authenticates, and one example is where we take our original IP header and data and authenticate it.

The only part that we don't authenticate is what's known as a mutable field. A mutable field changes as it moves; therefore, can you think of anything in an IP packet that changes while it is in transit?

You're correct if you think it's the TTL value or Time to Live because it decrements with each hop. As a result, this is a mutable field.

We're not going to authenticate that because if we route the packet from hop to hop and the TTL changes, the hash will make no sense when we recreate it on the other end and compare it. It's not going to work.

So, with AH, we can use transport mode or tunnel mode. Except for the mutable fields in the new IP header, AH has a new IP header and everything is authenticated. So that's an overview of ESP and AH, and we mostly use ESP these days because it supports Network Address Translation and connects us to the internet.

Everything we've discussed so far is considered a foundation component of VPN. So, in terms of core components, we have IPsec, which will provide me with certain building blocks, and we'll need to plug all of these building blocks in for the VPN to work.

So we need an ISAKMP policy, Diffie-Hellman keys, ESP, or AH, and we need to decide what kind of traffic should be encrypted. We can do this, for example, with an access control list. All of these little building blocks come together, and when we plug them all into our configuration, it forms an IPsec VPN, and we can now safely transmit our traffic across the network.

Many people say, "I have VPN" or "I use VPN," but they often don't understand what VPN is or what VPN-s can do for us.

As a result, I wanted to explain in a nutshell what a VPN is.

Just keep in mind that VPN consists of three components: confidentiality, data integrity, and data origin authentication. We talked about what makes all of that happen, the protocols, hash algorithms, key exchange methods, and security associations, and how when we put all of that together, all of those building blocks, they create a secure IPsec VPN.

9 783986 535384